Flávia Gonçalves Fernandes

Artificial Intelligence and Industry 4.0

Flávia Gonçalves Fernandes

Artificial Intelligence and Industry 4.0

Applications in Teaching, Research and Extension

ScienciaScripts

Imprint

Any brand names and product names mentioned in this book are subject to trademark, brand or patent protection and are trademarks or registered trademarks of their respective holders. The use of brand names, product names, common names, trade names, product descriptions etc. even without a particular marking in this work is in no way to be construed to mean that such names may be regarded as unrestricted in respect of trademark and brand protection legislation and could thus be used by anyone.

Cover image: www.ingimage.com

This book is a translation from the original published under ISBN 978-620-6-76072-6.

Publisher:
Sciencia Scripts
is a trademark of
Dodo Books Indian Ocean Ltd. and OmniScriptum S.R.L publishing group

120 High Road, East Finchley, London, N2 9ED, United Kingdom
Str. Armeneasca 28/1, office 1, Chisinau MD-2012, Republic of Moldova, Europe
Printed at: see last page
ISBN: 978-620-7-77249-0

FLÁVIA GONÇALVES FERNANDES

ARTIFICIAL INTELLIGENCE AND INDUSTRY 4.0: Applications in Teaching, Research and Extension

Table of contents

CHAPTER 1

RESEARCH PROJECT
AUTOMATION OF INDUSTRIAL PROCESSES USING ARTIFICIAL INTELLIGENCE

ABSTRACT: The Industry 4.0 revolution has brought significant advances in the automation and digitization of industrial processes. The integration of emerging technologies, such as Artificial Intelligence (AI), has the potential to transform manufacturing by increasing efficiency, improving quality control and optimizing production. This project aims to implement AI systems for automating manufacturing processes, with a focus on identifying patterns and anomalies in real time, contributing to productivity and reducing wasted resources. To achieve the proposed objectives, the methodology will be based on the development and application of neural networks and deep learning algorithms. The development of the project will be structured in phases over 36 months. The expected results of this project include an increase in productivity, a reduction in wasted resources, an improvement in quality control, technological progress, publications and dissemination of the objectives achieved, and the strengthening of links between industry, universities and innovation. This project not only aligns with the emerging trends of Industry 4.0, but also provides a solid basis for future research and development in the area of intelligent automation and optimization of industrial processes.

Keywords: automation, industry, artificial intelligence.

1. INTRODUCTION

The growing demand for efficiency and quality in manufacturing processes is driving the adoption of advanced technologies, such as Artificial Intelligence (AI), for industrial automation. Industry 4.0, characterized by the integration of cyber-physical systems, the Internet of Things (IoT) and big data, is transforming the way products are manufactured and operations are conducted. The intelligent automation of industrial processes, specifically through the implementation of AI systems, represents a significant evolution in this context.

Intelligent automation uses neural networks and deep learning algorithms to analyze data in real time, identify patterns and detect anomalies that could affect production. This approach not only increases productivity, but also reduces wasted resources, optimizes quality control and allows for more informed and accurate decision-making.

According to Lee et al. (2018), the application of AI in industrial automation has the potential to significantly transform manufacturing processes, providing greater flexibility and adaptability to variations in demand and product customization needs. In addition, the ability to monitor and adjust processes in real time contributes to maintaining quality and operational efficiency (ZHOU et al., 2015).

This research aims to implement AI systems for automating manufacturing processes, with a focus on optimizing production and quality control. The proposed methodology involves the development of neural networks and deep learning algorithms for identifying patterns and anomalies in real time. The application of these systems is expected to result in a significant increase in productivity and a substantial reduction in wasted resources, contributing to the sustainability and competitiveness of industrial operations.

2. JUSTIFICATION AND RELEVANCE

The application of AI in industrial processes is a response to the growing demand for efficiency and sustainability in manufacturing. With the use of neural networks and deep learning algorithms, it is possible not only to increase productivity, but also to significantly reduce the waste of resources, which is crucial for the competitiveness and sustainability of modern industries.

The intelligent automation of industrial processes, leveraged by Artificial Intelligence, represents an emerging frontier that promises to revolutionize manufacturing. The implementation of AI systems in industrial automation can significantly transform the efficiency and effectiveness of production processes. The use of neural networks and deep learning algorithms for quality control and production optimization is an innovative approach that makes it possible to identify patterns and anomalies in real time, resulting in greater productivity and reduced waste of resources (LEE et al., 2018; LU et al., 2020).

Industry 4.0, characterized by the integration of advanced digital technologies into manufacturing processes, relies heavily on AI to achieve its goals. Intelligent automation not only improves the accuracy and speed of operations, but also facilitates mass customization and predictive maintenance, reducing operating costs and minimizing unplanned downtime (KUSIAK, 2018).

This project aims to fill a significant gap in research into the practical application of AI in industrial environments. As well as providing valuable insights for the academic community, the expected results can be applied directly in industry, improving manufacturing processes and promoting technological innovation. Collaboration between universities and industries is crucial to develop robust solutions that are adaptable to market needs (WANG et al., 2016).

By increasing productivity and reducing the waste of resources, this project also contributes to environmental and economic sustainability. Companies that adopt these technologies not only become more competitive, but also more environmentally responsible, aligning themselves with global demands for sustainable practices (JESCHKE et al., 2017).

3. RELEVANCE OF THE TOPIC TO THE AREA IN WHICH THE PROPOSED PROJECT IS INSERTED

UNESP - Câmpus Itapeva currently offers two undergraduate programs: Industrial Wood Engineering and Production Engineering.

The Industrial Wood Engineering course, offered since the campus opened, also focuses on the development of technologies and processes, but with a specific emphasis on the wood industry. This course prepares students to work with the production, processing and use of wood products, contributing to innovation and efficiency in this area.

The Production Engineering course focuses on the area of Materials, including polymers, ceramics, metals and composites. Its aim is to provide knowledge for the development of products, processes and technologies applicable in various industries and companies providing services. It also aims to train professionals who are able to work in the areas of management, planning and control of industrial processes.

Both courses are designed to prepare students with the practical and theoretical skills needed to meet the contemporary challenges of their respective industries. The campus infrastructure includes well-equipped laboratories, modern classrooms and access to postgraduate programs in Mechanical Engineering in partnership with the Guaratinguetá Faculty of Engineering.

3.1. CONTEXTUALIZING INDUSTRY 4.0 AND THE IMPORTANCE OF AI IN INDUSTRIAL WOOD ENGINEERING

Industry 4.0, also known as the Fourth Industrial Revolution, is redefining production processes through the integration of advanced technologies such as the Internet of Things (IoT), cyber-physical systems and artificial intelligence (AI). In the manufacturing sector, these innovations promote a more intelligent and interconnected production environment, where machines and systems communicate and operate autonomously to optimize efficiency and productivity (KAGERMANN et al., 2013).

In the context of Industrial Wood Engineering, the application of AI is particularly significant. AI can be used to automate manufacturing processes, control quality and optimize production, bringing substantial benefits to the timber industry, which traditionally faces challenges related to the variability of raw materials and the need for precision in cutting and finishing. The use of deep learning algorithms and neural networks enables real-time analysis of production data, identifying patterns and anomalies that can be corrected autonomously, resulting in increased efficiency and reduced waste of resources (LIU et al., 2019).

The adoption of Industry 4.0 technologies in Industrial Wood Engineering involves the development of intelligent systems that can monitor and adjust production processes automatically. For example, integrated IoT sensors can provide continuous data on machine operating conditions and product quality, while AI algorithms can analyze this data to predict failures and suggest necessary adjustments for optimization. Studies show that this approach not only improves the quality of the end product, but also reduces operating costs and minimizes environmental impacts by decreasing resource consumption (LEE et al., 2018).

In addition, the implementation of AI in the timber industry can contribute to sustainability by promoting more efficient practices and less waste. The ability to adjust production processes in real time based on accurate and up-to-date data ensures greater adaptability to market demands and variations in material properties (HE et al., 2020).

Therefore, integrating AI into Industrial Wood Engineering not only improves productivity and efficiency, but also prepares the sector to face future challenges, ensuring sustainable and competitive development.

3.2. CONTEXTUALIZING INDUSTRY 4.0 AND THE IMPORTANCE OF AI IN PRODUCTION ENGINEERING

Industry 4.0 represents a significant transformation in manufacturing, characterized by the integration of digital technologies and cyber-physical systems into production processes. This paradigm aims to create smart factories where machines and systems communicate and cooperate autonomously, resulting in greater efficiency, flexibility and customization in production. Advanced automation and real-time data analysis are key to this evolution, enabling a rapid response to market demands and changes in the production environment (KAGERMANN et al., 2013).

A central component of Industry 4.0 is the application of Artificial Intelligence (AI), which enables the intelligent automation of industrial processes. AI, particularly through neural networks and deep learning algorithms, plays a crucial role in optimizing manufacturing processes. These technologies enable the analysis and interpretation of large volumes of data generated by sensors and IoT devices, identifying patterns and anomalies that can be used to improve production quality and efficiency (LEE et al., 2018).

In the context of Production Engineering, AI offers several advantages, such as the automation of complex tasks and the implementation of quality control systems based on computer vision and machine learning. Studies show that the use of convolutional neural networks (CNNs) can significantly increase accuracy in detecting product defects, surpassing traditional inspection methods (Liu et al., 2019). In addition, process optimization through deep learning algorithms contributes to reducing waste and maximizing operational efficiency (HE et al., 2020).

The integration of AI into Production Engineering not only increases productivity, but also promotes sustainability by reducing resource consumption and minimizing the environmental impact of industrial operations. The ability to adjust production parameters in real time, based on accurate and up-to-date data, allows for quick and efficient adaptation to market variables, providing a significant competitive advantage (SCHWABACHER & GOEBEL, 2007).

Therefore, intelligent automation, driven by AI, is essential for the modernization of manufacturing in Industry 4.0. The implementation of AI systems in industrial processes represents a crucial technological advance that transforms the way products are manufactured and operations are managed, promoting an era of smarter, more efficient and sustainable production.

4. CLARITY, RELEVANCE, ORIGINALITY AND JUSTIFICATION OF OBJECTIVES

4.1. GENERAL OBJECTIVE

The overall aim of this project is to implement artificial intelligence (AI) systems for automating manufacturing processes. This includes the development of technologies for quality control and production optimization, with the aim of increasing productivity and reducing the waste of resources in industrial operations.

4.2. SPECIFIC OBJECTIVES

In order to achieve the main objective of this research project, the specific objectives listed below were stipulated:

- Create and train artificial neural networks that can analyze manufacturing data in real time, identifying operational patterns and anomalies;

- Developing deep learning algorithms capable of automatically predicting and adjusting production processes, improving operational efficiency;

- Establishing AI systems for continuous monitoring of product quality, identifying defects and ensuring compliance with established standards;

- Implementing AI solutions to optimize processes, minimizing the waste of materials and energy resources and maximizing productivity;

- Incorporate sensors and IoT devices to collect data in real time, allowing for a more accurate and detailed analysis of the manufacturing environment.

4.3. CLARITY OF OBJECTIVES

The overall objective of this project is clearly defined: to implement AI systems for automating manufacturing processes, including quality control and production optimization. This objective is broken down into specific actions, such as the development of neural networks and deep learning algorithms to identify patterns and anomalies in real time. The focus is on improving operational efficiency and reducing waste, which makes the objectives tangible and measurable.

4.4.   RELEVANCE OF OBJECTIVES

The relevance of this project's objectives is reflected in its direct connection with the contemporary needs of industry. Industry 4.0 emphasizes the integration of advanced technologies, such as AI, to improve industrial processes. In this context, the intelligent automation of manufacturing processes is crucial to maintaining the competitiveness and sustainability of industrial operations. In addition, production optimization and quality control are essential aspects for any manufacturing sector, ensuring that products meet market standards and reducing operating costs.

4.5.   ORIGINALITY OF OBJECTIVES

The originality of this project lies in the innovative application of AI specifically to manufacturing processes. While many studies and projects focus on the automation of industrial processes in general, this project distinguishes itself by integrating deep learning algorithms for real-time analysis of data collected directly from the manufacturing environment. This approach not only modernizes traditional processes, but also introduces new ways of identifying and solving operational problems before they impact production, creating a proactive and self-sustaining manufacturing system.

4.6.   RATIONALE FOR THE OBJECTIVES

The project's objectives are well grounded in current industry trends and needs. Recent literature and studies point to the growing importance of AI in industrial automation. According to research by Lee et al. (2018), the implementation of AI technologies in manufacturing can lead to a reduction of up to 30% in operating costs and a 25% increase in production efficiency. In addition, the proposed approach is in line with Industry 4.0 guidelines, which emphasize the need for intelligent and connected systems to improve flexibility and customization in production (KAGERMANN et al., 2013).

By basing the objectives on concrete data and trends, the project not only demonstrates its feasibility, but also its relevance and potential positive impact on the industrial sector. This combination of clarity, relevance, originality and robust rationale underlines the project's importance and promise for significant advances in industrial automation.

5. THEORETICAL FOUNDATION AND COHERENCE OF THE METHODS USED WITH THE PROPOSED OBJECTIVES

5.1. INDUSTRY 4.0

Industry 4.0, also known as the Fourth Industrial Revolution, represents a profound transformation in industrial processes, driven by the integration of advanced digital technologies. It is characterized by the fusion of cyber-physical systems, the Internet of Things (IoT), big data and artificial intelligence (AI), creating smart and highly connected factories (LEE et al., 2018).

The concept of Industry 4.0 emerged in Germany as part of a strategic plan to modernize manufacturing and increase global competitiveness. This new industrial era aims to automate and digitize production processes, allowing for greater flexibility, efficiency and mass customization of products (ZHOU et al., 2015).

One of the main characteristics of Industry 4.0 is the ability to collect and analyze data in real time, using sensors and connected devices to monitor and optimize each stage of production. AI plays a crucial role in this context, providing control systems and predictive analysis that help anticipate problems and improve product quality (LU, 2017).

The integration of these technologies results in a significant increase in productivity and operational efficiency, while reducing the waste of resources and improving the sustainability of industrial operations. Intelligent automation, through neural networks and deep learning algorithms, enables the identification of patterns and anomalies, optimizing quality control and decision-making (LEE et al., 2018).

In short, Industry 4.0 represents a significant advance in the way industrial processes are managed and executed, offering unprecedented opportunities for innovation and continuous improvement.

5.2. ARTIFICIAL INTELLIGENCE

Artificial Intelligence (AI) is a field of computer science dedicated to developing systems capable of performing tasks that traditionally require human intelligence. These tasks range from analyzing data to making complex decisions. AI seeks to replicate the capacity for learning, reasoning, problem-solving and decision-making that characterizes human thought.

One of the most fascinating features of AI is its ability to learn from data. This ability is exploited through techniques such as Machine Learning, which allows systems to improve their performance on certain tasks as they are exposed to more data. Another crucial technique is the use of Artificial Neural Networks, which are computer models inspired by the structure of the human brain and are capable of learning complex patterns in data.

In industry, AI is playing an increasingly important role in automating processes and optimizing production. Machine Learning, for example, can be applied to predict market demands, optimize supply chains and even prevent equipment failures. Artificial Neural Networks are used in quality control systems, identifying patterns in images and videos, and in diagnostic and predictive maintenance processes.

In addition, other AI techniques such as Natural Language Processing

(NLP) are used to analyze texts and human-machine interaction through natural language. This makes it possible, for example, to automate customer service processes and extract insights from large volumes of textual data.

Computer Vision is another powerful technique that allows machines to understand and interpret the visual world, and is used in object recognition systems, product fault detection, and even autonomous vehicles.

In short, Artificial Intelligence is revolutionizing industry by offering tools and techniques capable of automating processes, increasing operational efficiency and providing valuable insights from data, thus contributing to the advancement and competitiveness of businesses in an increasingly digitalized world.

AI is therefore increasingly important in various areas of modern society due to its ability to transform processes, improve efficiency and promote innovation. It has become a significant driving force in several areas, including industry, health, finance and transportation.

Here are some aspects that highlight the importance of AI today (BRYNJOLFSSON; MCAFEE, 2014; RUSSELL; NORVIG, 2020; DOMINGOS, 2015):

- **Process automation:** AI makes it possible to automate repetitive and routine tasks, allowing human workers to focus on more complex and creative activities. This is particularly relevant in sectors such as manufacturing, where automation can significantly increase productivity and reduce errors.

- **Improved Decision Making:** AI systems are capable of analyzing large volumes of data in real time, offering insights that help with strategic decision-making. In sectors such as finance, health and logistics, this can lead to more informed and accurate decisions.

- **Personalization of Services:** AI enables the personalization of services on an unprecedented scale. For example, in digital marketing, AI algorithms can analyze consumer behavior and offer personalized recommendations, increasing customer satisfaction and sales.

- **Advances in Health:** In the field of health, AI is revolutionizing the diagnosis and treatment of diseases. Machine learning algorithms can analyze medical images to detect diseases more accurately and at earlier stages than traditional methods. In addition, AI is being used to develop personalized treatments and new drugs.

- **Improving Security:** AI plays a crucial role in cyber security, helping to detect and respond to threats in real time. In addition, AI-equipped surveillance systems can improve public safety by analyzing video in real time to identify suspicious behavior.

- **Economic Impact:** AI has a significant impact on the global economy, driving innovation and competitiveness. Companies that adopt AI can gain significant competitive advantages by increasing operational efficiency and creating new business models.

- **Education and Research:** AI is transforming education by personalizing learning for each student. Adaptive learning platforms use AI to identify students' individual needs and offer specific content to improve learning.

- **Industry 4.0:** In the context of Industry 4.0, AI is key to creating smart factories. AI systems can monitor and optimize operations in real time, predict equipment failures and improve product quality, resulting in greater efficiency and less waste.

In short, AI is playing a crucial role in technological advancement and the transformation of multiple sectors, bringing benefits ranging from improved operational efficiency to the personalization of services and advances in healthcare. Its continued implementation promises to shape the future in significant ways.

5.3. APPLICATION OF ARTIFICIAL INTELLIGENCE IN INDUSTRY 4.0

In the context of Industry 4.0, AI is key to intelligent automation and the creation of connected and efficient factories, among other applications such as:

- **Real-time monitoring:** AI enables continuous monitoring of industrial processes, identifying anomalies and patterns that may indicate future problems or opportunities for improvement (LEE et al., 2018);

- **Production Optimization:** Deep learning algorithms can optimize production processes, adjusting parameters in real time to maximize efficiency and minimize waste (ZHOU et al., 2015);

- **Quality Control:** AI can be used to inspect products accurately, ensuring high quality standards and reducing costs associated with defects (LU, 2017);

- **Predictive Maintenance:** With predictive analytics, AI can predict equipment failures before they occur, enabling proactive maintenance and reducing downtime (JESCHKE et al., 2017);

- **Automation and Efficiency:** AI enables the automation of repetitive and complex tasks, increasing efficiency and reducing human error. This is essential for competitiveness in a globalized market (MCKINSEY; COMPANY, 2018);

- **Data Analysis:** With the ability to process large volumes of data in real time, AI provides valuable insights that can improve decision-making and product innovation (BIESINGER et al., 2020);

- **Innovation:** AI drives innovation by enabling new ways of solving problems, from predicting failures to developing customized products (RUSSELL; NORVIG, 2021).

In short, AI is a crucial component of Industry 4.0, offering benefits ranging from automation and optimization of production processes to continuous innovation and quality improvement. Its application in industry transforms not only internal operations, but also the way companies interact with the market and adapt to change.

5.4. INDUSTRIAL AUTOMATION

Industrial Automation represents a significant advance in the way companies operate and manage their production processes. It involves the use of systems and technologies to control and operate industrial processes in an automated way, reducing the need for direct human intervention. This field covers a wide range of applications, from controlling simple processes to operating entire factories autonomously (HE et al., 2020).

There are different types of industrial automation, each with its own objectives and specific applications. Process automation refers to the automation of sequential and repetitive steps in a production line, such as the assembly of components in a car factory. Machine automation refers to the incorporation of automatic devices into industrial equipment to perform specific tasks, such as welding robots on metal production lines. Control automation deals with the automated monitoring and management of industrial processes, ensuring that they operate within predefined and safe parameters (SCHWABACHER; GOEBEL, 2007).

The advantages of industrial automation are diverse and have a positive impact on companies' efficiency and competitiveness. Firstly, automation helps to reduce operating costs by eliminating the need for human labor in repetitive and error-prone tasks. In addition, automation increases productivity by allowing machines to perform tasks faster and more efficiently than human workers (LIU et al., 2019).

Improving product quality is another significant advantage of industrial automation. By replacing manual intervention with automated processes, automation reduces variability and human error, resulting in more consistent and better quality products. In addition, automation provides greater operational flexibility, allowing companies to quickly adjust production to meet market demands and introduce new products more quickly (LEE et al., 2018).

Finally, industrial automation also contributes to safety in the workplace, reducing workers' exposure to dangerous environments and minimizing the risk of accidents. By implementing robust and reliable automation systems, companies can guarantee a safer and healthier working environment for their employees (BOGUE, 2017).

In short, industrial automation is a powerful tool for increasing efficiency, quality and safety in production processes, resulting in tangible benefits for companies and the economy as a whole. By adopting automation technologies, companies can remain competitive in an increasingly dynamic and demanding global market.

5.5. INDUSTRIAL AUTOMATION USING ARTIFICIAL INTELLIGENCE

Intelligent automation of industrial processes has become a fundamental pillar in Industry 4.0, leveraging advances in Artificial Intelligence to transform manufacturing operations. Industry 4.0, characterized by the integration of digital technologies into industrial processes, promises to optimize production, improve product quality and reduce waste. The use of AI, specifically neural networks and deep learning algorithms, makes it possible to identify patterns and anomalies in real time, which is essential for advanced automation and quality control.

Intelligent industrial automation involves using AI systems to automate tasks that previously required human intervention. This includes monitoring and controlling manufacturing processes to ensure that products are manufactured with high quality and efficiency. According to Lee et al. (2018), the application of neural networks in industrial processes has demonstrated a significant ability to predict failures and optimize the operation of equipment, which directly contributes to improving operational efficiency.

One of the main components of this transformation is the use of *deep learning*, which allows AI systems to learn from large volumes of data from sensors and other IoT (Internet of Things) devices. This is vital for the early detection of anomalies and predictive maintenance, areas where AI can predict problems before they occur and thus minimize machine downtime (SCHWABACHER; GOEBEL, 2007).

In addition, integrating AI into manufacturing processes facilitates real-time optimization, automatically adjusting operating parameters to maximize efficiency. This dynamic adjustment capability is essential for responding quickly to production variables and market demand (HE et al., 2020). An interdisciplinary approach, combining knowledge of production engineering and industrial wood engineering, is crucial to developing practical and effective solutions in the context of Industry 4.0.

In the area of quality control, convolutional neural networks (CNNs) have been widely used for product inspection, ensuring that each item produced meets established standards. Liu et al. (2019) point out that CNNs can detect defects on material surfaces with greater accuracy than traditional methods, demonstrating the potential of AI to revolutionize industrial quality control.

The development of AI systems for intelligent automation must also consider scalability and integration with existing systems. This involves creating flexible platforms that can be adapted to the specific needs of different industries. According to Bogue (2017), modularity and interoperability are critical aspects that must be incorporated into the design of automation solutions to ensure their broad and sustainable applicability.

In short, the intelligent automation of industrial processes, based on AI and Industry 4.0 technologies, represents a significant advance in modern manufacturing. The implementation of these technologies promises not only to increase productivity and efficiency, but also to reduce waste, promote sustainability and improve product quality. Studies and practical applications in various industrial sectors confirm the transformative potential of these innovations, paving the way for a future of smarter, more integrated production.

6. METHODOLOGY

The methodology of this project involves the application of advanced artificial intelligence (AI) techniques for the automation and optimization of manufacturing processes. The central objective is to implement AI systems that can carry out quality control and production optimization in real time, guaranteeing greater efficiency and reducing waste. This project will therefore be developed through several phases, described below.

6.1. STEP 1: LITERATURE REVIEW AND INITIAL PLANNING

In this stage, a comprehensive review of existing literature on industrial process automation and the use of artificial intelligence (AI) in manufacturing will be carried out. The review will include academic articles, technical publications and case studies that document best practices and emerging technologies in the field. Based on this review, a detailed project plan will be drawn up, defining the specific objectives, the methodological approach and the schedule of activities.

6.2. STAGE 2: DATA COLLECTION AND PRE-PROCESSING

In order to develop effective AI models, it is essential to have high-quality data. In this stage, relevant data sources will be identified and implemented, such as production line sensors and quality control systems. The data collected will be pre-processed to ensure its integrity and usefulness, including steps such as cleaning, normalization and treatment of missing values. In addition, relevant features will be selected to feed the AI models.

6.3. STEP 3: DEVELOPING IA MODELS

With the data ready, the development of AI models begins. In this phase, neural networks and deep learning algorithms will be designed and trained to identify patterns and anomalies in manufacturing processes in real time. Supervised and unsupervised learning techniques will be applied to create robust models. The training phase will include dividing the data into training and test sets to validate the accuracy and generalizability of the models.

6.4. STEP 4: IMPLEMENTATION AND INTEGRATION

Once the AI models have been developed and validated, the next step is to implement them in a production environment. The models will be integrated into existing manufacturing systems, such as quality control and production optimization systems. Pilot tests will be carried out to ensure that the models work correctly in a real environment and that they can be monitored and adjusted as necessary.

6.5. STEP 5: MONITORING AND OPTIMIZATION

After implementation, the performance of the AI systems will be monitored on an ongoing basis. This stage involves continuously collecting production data to detect any deviations or anomalies. The feedback will be used to make adjustments and optimizations to the models, ensuring that they continue to improve productivity and reduce wasted resources. In addition, new opportunities for applying AI will be explored to expand the benefits of intelligent automation.

This methodology proposes a robust and practical approach to the intelligent automation of industrial processes, combining the most advanced AI technologies with a careful implementation strategy to maximize the benefits and minimize the associated risks.

7. ADEQUACY OF THE PROJECT TO THE GROUP(S) AND LINE(S) OF RESEARCH OF THE DEPARTMENT/COURSE COORDINATOR

The project to automate industrial processes using artificial intelligence (AI) is aligned in a robust and integrated way with the lines of research of the Simulation and Computational Modeling Group of the Department/Coordination of Courses. The proposal to implement AI systems for automating manufacturing processes, including quality control and production optimization, offers synergy with the group's various areas of activity.

7.1. ALIGNMENT WITH LINES OF RESEARCH

7.1.1. Machine Learning and Data Mining

The development of neural networks and deep learning algorithms is a central component of machine learning. This project involves creating models that can learn and identify patterns in real-time manufacturing data, which is directly relevant to the line of research in machine learning and data mining.

7.1.2. Statistical and Computational Methods with Applications in Physics and Engineering

The use of advanced statistical methods is essential for analyzing large volumes of data generated by industrial processes. The application of computational methods to model and simulate production processes helps to optimize AI algorithms.

7.1.3. Numerical/Computational Modeling of Structures and Materials

Numerical modeling is essential for simulating industrial processes and predicting the performance of AI systems. This project can use computer modeling techniques to create accurate simulations of manufacturing processes, allowing for continuous optimization.

7.1.4. Game Theory: Classical and Quantum Case

Game theory can be applied to optimize decisions in manufacturing environments, where multiple agents (machines, AI systems) interact and compete for resources. Although this is not the main focus of the project, there is potential to explore these interactions using game theory frameworks.

7.2. CONTRIBUTIONS TO THE RESEARCH GROUP

This project will bring several significant contributions to the Simulation and Computational Modeling Group, including:

- **Advances in AI Algorithms:** Development of advanced deep learning algorithms that can be applied in other areas of the group's research.
- **Multidisciplinary Integration:** Encouraging interdisciplinary

collaboration, integrating knowledge of physics, engineering, computer science and statistics.

- **Practical Applications:** Creation of practical applications that can be implemented in industry, strengthening the connection between academic research and industrial needs.

- **Publications and Scientific Dissemination:** The project has a high potential for generating high-impact publications in renowned scientific journals and conferences.

The project of automating industrial processes using AI is perfectly suited to the research lines of the Simulation and Computational Modeling Group. It not only complements existing areas of study, but also offers new opportunities for innovation and practical application, promoting the advancement of knowledge and interdisciplinary collaboration.

8. PHYSICAL AND FINANCIAL TIMETABLE

8.1. WORK PLAN AND EXECUTION SCHEDULE

8.1.1. Stage 1: Literature Review and Initial Planning (Months 1-3)

Activities:

- Bibliographical research on neural networks and deep learning.
- Case studies of successful implementation of AI in manufacturing.
- Definition of project parameters and requirements.

Timeline:

- Month 1: Literature review and definition of scope.
- Month 2: Identification of success stories and project parameters.
- Month 3: Finalization of initial planning.

8.1.2. Stage 2: Data Collection and Pre-processing (Months 4-9)

Activities:

- Installation of IoT sensors and integration with control systems.
- Real-time and historical data collection.
- Data cleaning and normalization.

Timeline:

- Month 4: Sensor installation and initial integration.
- Month 5-6: Collection of historical and real-time data.
- Month 7-9: Data cleaning and normalization.

8.1.3. Stage 3: Developing AI Models (Months 10-24)

Activities:

- Creation and training of artificial neural network models.
- Development of *deep learning* models.
- Model validation and adjustment.

Timeline:

- Month 10-12: Initial creation of AI models.
- Month 13-18: Training and development of advanced models.
- Month 19-24: Model validation and adjustments.

8.1.4. Stage 4: Implementation and Integration (Months 25-30)

Activities:

- Integration of AI models with manufacturing control systems.
- Tests in a controlled environment.
- Adjustments based on feedback.

Timeline:

- Month 25-27: Integration and initial tests.
- Month 28-30: Adjustments based on feedback.

8.1.5. Stage 5: Monitoring and Optimization (Months 31-36)

Activities:

- Implementation of dashboards and alert systems.
- Continuous feedback collection and model adjustment.
- Updating the models with new data.

Timeline:

- Month 31-33: Implementation of monitoring systems.
- Month 34-36: Collecting feedback and updating the models.

8.2. MATERIALS AND RESOURCES

8.2.1. Servers and Computing Infrastructure

- High-performance servers for training AI models;
- Data storage (high-capacity HDDs and SSDs);
- Backup systems and data security.

8.2.2. Software and licenses

- Software licenses for AI development (TensorFlow, PyTorch);
- Data analysis tools (Matlab, R, Python);
- Database management systems (SQL Server, MongoDB).

8.2.3. Sensors and Data Collection Equipment

- Industrial sensors for real-time data collection (temperature, pressure, speed, etc.);
- Sensor interface equipment (PLCs, data acquisition modules).

8.2.4. Prototype development and testing

- Electronic prototyping kits (Arduino, Raspberry Pi);
- Assembly and welding tools;
- Various electronic components (resistors, capacitors, transistors).

8.2.5. Network infrastructure

- Network equipment (routers, switches, network cables);
- Cloud services for storage and processing (AWS, Google Cloud).

8.2.6. Human Resources

- Team made up of research professors, laboratory technicians and undergraduate and postgraduate students from UNESP - Câmpus Itapeva.

8.3.   FINANCIAL BUDGET

8.3.1. Servers and Computing Infrastructure

- High-performance servers: R$ 100,000.00
- Data storage: R$ 50.000,00
- Backup and data security systems: R$ 30,000.00
Subtotal: R$ 180,000.00

8.3.2. Software and licenses

- AI software licenses: R$ 40,000.00
- Data analysis tools: R$ 30.000,00
- Database management systems: R$ 20,000.00
  Subtotal: R$ 90,000.00

8.3.3. Sensors and Data Collection Equipment

- Industrial sensors: R$ 50,000.00
- Sensor interface equipment: R$ 20,000.00
Subtotal: R$ 70,000.00

8.3.4. Prototype development and testing

- Electronic prototyping kits: R$ 10,000.00
- Assembly and welding tools: R$ 5,000.00
- Miscellaneous electronic components: R$ 15,000.00
Subtotal: R$ 30,000.00

8.3.5. Network infrastructure

- Network equipment: R$ 20,000.00

- Cloud services: R$ 50,000.00

Subtotal: R$ 70,000.00

8.3.6. Human Resources

Undergraduate scholarships (4 students): R$ 150.000,00

Postgraduate scholarships (2 students): R$ 160.000,00

Subtotal: R$ 310,000.00

TOTAL: 750.000,00

This budget is an initial estimate and may vary depending on the specifics of the project and the need to adapt over the 36-month period. The efficient allocation of resources and the continuous evaluation of costs and benefits will guarantee the successful implementation of the intelligent industrial process automation system.

8.3.7. Budget Justification

Implementing AI systems to automate manufacturing processes requires a robust and up-to-date infrastructure. High-performance servers and network infrastructure are essential for real-time processing and analysis of the data collected. Software licenses are required for the development and implementation of AI algorithms, while industrial sensors ensure the accurate collection of data from the manufacturing environment.

Human resources represent a significant part of the budget, reflecting the need for specialists in various areas to ensure the success of the project. Investment in developing and testing prototypes is crucial in order to validate the proposed solutions before they are implemented on a large scale.

The proposed budget is detailed and justified, ensuring that all critical aspects of the project are covered, from the technological infrastructure to the human talent needed to develop and implement the AI solutions.

9. EXEQUIBILITY

The implementation of artificial intelligence (AI) systems for the automation of industrial processes is a viable and necessary proposal for the modernization of manufacturing. This project aims to integrate neural networks and deep learning algorithms into quality control and production optimization, increasing productivity and reducing wasted resources. The feasibility of the project is supported by the growing maturity of AI technologies and the availability of adequate technological infrastructure.

9.1. TECHNICAL FEASIBILITY

AI technologies, especially neural networks and deep learning algorithms, have proven highly effective at identifying patterns and anomalies in real time. The literature points to several successful applications of AI in industrial environments, suggesting that the necessary technical components are available and affordable.

Neural Networks and Deep Learning: Convolutional neural networks (CNNs) and recurrent neural networks (RNNs) have been widely used in computer vision and time series analysis applications, respectively. These technologies are particularly useful for product defect detection and predictive maintenance forecasting (LECUN; BENGIO; HINTON, 2015; SCHMIDHUBER, 2015).

Computing Infrastructure: The availability of specialized hardware, such as graphics processing units (GPUs) and tensor processing units (TPUs), enables the efficient execution of AI algorithms. Cloud computing platforms such as AWS, Google Cloud and Microsoft Azure also offer scalable services for training and implementing AI models.

9.2. ECONOMIC VIABILITY

Adopting AI in industrial processes can initially involve a significant investment in technology and training. However, the medium and long-term benefits, such as improved operational efficiency and reduced waste, justify the investment. Studies indicate that intelligent automation can increase productivity by up to 30% and reduce operating costs by up to 20% (MCKINSEY GLOBAL INSTITUTE, 2017).

9.3. OPERATIONAL VIABILITY

Implementing AI in industrial processes requires a collaborative environment where production engineers and AI specialists work together. The integration of AI systems with existing control systems can be managed through a phased approach, minimizing interruptions in production.

Intelligent automation of industrial processes using AI is both technically and economically feasible. With proper planning and collaboration between different areas of expertise, the implementation of this project can result in significant advances in operational efficiency and waste reduction, contributing to the competitiveness and sustainability of the manufacturing industry.

10. EXPECTED RESULTS

The Intelligent Automation of Industrial Processes project aims to implement Artificial Intelligence (AI) systems for automating manufacturing processes, with a focus on quality control and production optimization. The expected results include:

10.1. INCREASED PRODUCTIVITY

- **Reduced Production Time:** Through intelligent automation, a significant acceleration in manufacturing processes is expected, resulting in greater productivity.
- **Operational Efficiency:** Automation enables continuous and more efficient machine operation, minimizing downtime and bottlenecks in production.

10.2. IMPROVED QUALITY CONTROL

- **Real-time anomaly detection:** The use of neural networks and deep learning algorithms will enable immediate identification of defects and anomalies in products, guaranteeing more rigorous and precise quality control.
- **Reducing Human Errors:** Automating quality control will reduce dependence on manual inspections, minimizing human errors and inconsistencies.

10.3. PRODUCTION OPTIMIZATION

- **Identifying Production Patterns:** Real-time data analysis will make it possible to identify patterns and trends that can be used to optimize production processes.
- **Dynamic Parameter Adjustment:** AI systems will be able to automatically adjust production parameters based on collected data, improving efficiency and product quality.

10.4. REDUCED WASTE OF RESOURCES

- **Efficient Use of Materials:** Intelligent automation will help to use materials more efficiently, reducing waste and associated costs.
- **Minimizing Energy Waste:** Optimizing processes will result in lower energy consumption, contributing to more sustainable production practices.

10.5. DEVELOPING SKILLS AND KNOWLEDGE

- **Training Professionals:** The implementation and operation of AI systems will require the training of engineers and technicians, promoting the development of advanced skills in AI and automation.
- **Academic integration:** The results and methodologies of the project can be integrated into the curriculum of the Production Engineering and

Industrial Wood Engineering courses, promoting education that is more in line with the needs of Industry 4.0.

10.6. EXPECTED IMPACT

The positive impacts of the project include the strengthening of ties between universities and industry, as well as a significant increase in the competitiveness of national manufacturing, promoting more efficient and sustainable production. Through the adoption of AI technologies, it is also hoped to foster innovation in the industrial sector, providing economic and environmental advantages. In addition, the development of technical skills in AI and automation among professionals and students will contribute to the formation of a more qualified workforce prepared for the challenges of Industry 4.0.

REFERENCES

BIESINGER, F.; WEYRICH, M.; MEISEN, T. **Artificial Intelligence in Industry 4.0 and its Impact on Supply Chains**. Procedia CIRP, v. 93, p. 161-165, 2020.

BOGUE, R. **What are the prospects for robots in the factory? Part 1**. Industrial Robot: An International Journal, 2017.

BRYNJOLFSSON, E.; MCAFEE, A. **The Second Machine Age**: Work, Progress, and Prosperity in a Time of Brilliant Technologies. New York: W.W. Norton & Company, 2014.

DOMINGOS, P. **The Master Algorithm**: How the Quest for the Ultimate Learning Machine Will Remake Our World. New York: Basic Books, 2015.

GOODFELLOW, I.; BENGIO, Y.; COURVILLE, A. **Deep Learning**. Cambridge: MIT Press, 2016.

HASTIE, T.; TIBSHIRANI, R.; FRIEDMAN, J. **The Elements of Statistical Learning**: Data Mining, Inference, and Prediction. 2. ed. New York: Springer, 2009.

HE, Y.; XU, X.; WANG, Z.; JIANG, Y. **Predictive Maintenance in Smart Manufacturing**: A Review. IEEE Transactions on Industrial Informatics, 2020.

HUGHES, T. J. **The Finite Element Method**: Linear Static and Dynamic Finite Element Analysis. 2. ed. New York: Courier Corporation, 2012.

JESCHKE, S.; BRECHER, C.; MEISEN, T.; ÖZDEMIR, D.; ESCHERT, T. **Industrial Internet of Things and Cyber Manufacturing Systems**. New York: Springer, 2017.

JORDAN, M. I.; MITCHELL, T. M. **Machine Learning**: Trends, Perspectives, and Prospects. Science, v. 349, n. 6245, p. 255-260, 2015.

KAGERMANN, H.; WAHLSTER, W.; HELBIG, J. **Recommendations for Implementing the Strategic Initiative INDUSTRIE 4.0**: Securing the Future of German Manufacturing Industry. 2013.

KAGERMANN, H.; WAHLSTER, W.; HELBIG, J. **Recommendations for Implementing the Strategic Initiative INDUSTRIE 4.0**. Final Report of the Industrie 4.0 Working Group, 2013.

KUSIAK, A. **Smart Manufacturing**. International Journal of Production Research, v. 56, n. 1-2, p. 508-517, 2018.

LECUN, Y.; BENGIO, Y.; HINTON, G. **Deep Learning**. Nature, v. 521, n. 7553, p. 436-444, 2015.

LEE, J.; BAGHERI, B.; KAO, H. A. **A Cyber-Physical Systems Architecture for Industry 4.0-Based Manufacturing Systems**. Manufacturing Letters, v. 3, p. 18-23, 2018.

LIU, C.; LIU, P.; JIANG, L. **Surface Defect Detection of Industrial Products Based on Deep Learning**. Journal of Intelligent Manufacturing, 2019.

MCKINSEY & COMPANY. **Artificial Intelligence**: The Next Digital Frontier?. 2018.

OSBORNE, M. J.; RUBINSTEIN, A. **A Course in Game Theory**. Cambridge: MIT Press, 1994.

RUSSELL, S.; NORVIG, P. **Artificial Intelligence**: A Modern Approach. 4. ed. New York: Pearson, 2020.

RUSSELL, S.; NORVIG, P. **Artificial Intelligence**: A Modern Approach. 5. ed. New York: Pearson, 2021.

SCHMIDHUBER, J. **Deep Learning in Neural Networks**: An Overview. Neural Networks, v. 61, p. 85-117, 2015.

SCHWABACHER, M.; GOEBEL, K. **A Survey of Artificial Intelligence for Prognostics**. AAAI Fall Symposium - Technical Report, 2007.

WANG, S.; WAN, J.; LI, D.; ZHANG, C. **Implementing Smart Factory of Industrie 4.0**: An Outlook. International Journal of Distributed Sensor Networks, v. 12, n. 1, p. 3159805, 2016.

ZHANG, Y.; REN, S.; LIU, Y.; SI, S. **A Big Data Analytics Architecture for Cleaner Manufacturing and Maintenance Processes of Complex Products**. Journal of Cleaner Production, v. 142, p. 626-641, 2017.

ZHOU, K.; LIU, T.; ZHOU, L. **Industry 4.0**: Towards Future Industrial Opportunities and Challenges. In: 12th International Conference on Fuzzy Systems and Knowledge Discovery (FSKD). 2015. p. 2147-2152.

CHAPTER 2

UNIVERSITY EXTENSION ACTION PLAN
UNIVERSITY-INDUSTRY INTEGRATION: DRIVING AUTOMATION WITH ARTIFICIAL INTELLIGENCE

ABSTRACT: The extension project "University-Industry Integration: Boosting Automation with Artificial Intelligence" aims to integrate the university and the local industrial community through the implementation of artificial intelligence (AI) systems for automating manufacturing processes, quality control and production optimization. Using a structured methodology, the project aims to disseminate knowledge about AI and Industry 4.0, train industry professionals in AI techniques, develop partnerships between the university and companies in the sector, and hold workshops and seminars on the practical application of AI in industry. With adequate financial resources, significant results are expected to be achieved, including the training of professionals and students, the successful implementation of intelligent automation systems, the reduction of waste and increased productivity in partner industries, and the strengthening of partnerships between the university and the industrial sector. Through these initiatives, the project aims to promote innovations that benefit both the university and the industrial community, contributing to the advancement of knowledge and the sustainable development of regional industry.

Keywords: automation, industry, artificial intelligence.

11. INTRODUCTION

The intelligent automation of industrial processes represents one of the fundamental pillars of Industry 4.0, characterized by the integration of advanced technologies such as artificial intelligence (AI) into manufacturing environments. This movement aims to transform traditional factories into intelligent production systems, capable of adapting quickly to market changes and significantly improving operational efficiency. AI, through deep learning techniques and neural networks, offers powerful tools for quality control, production optimization and the identification of anomalies in real time.

With this in mind, the main aim of this project is to promote close integration between the university and the local industrial community through extension activities aimed at implementing artificial intelligence (AI) systems in industry.

Recognizing the growing importance of AI and Industry 4.0 in today's industrial context, this project aims not only to disseminate knowledge about these areas, but also to train industry professionals in AI techniques applied to process automation, quality control and production optimization.

In addition, the aim is to develop solid partnerships between the university and companies in the industrial sector, with a view to strategic collaborations that boost innovation and regional economic development. Through workshops, seminars and pilot projects, the aim is to provide a practical and tangible application of AI in local industry, thus promoting the adoption of innovative technologies that contribute to the continuous improvement of industrial processes and strengthening the competitiveness of local companies.

12. TARGET AUDIENCE

The target audience for this project is:

- Students of production engineering and industrial wood engineering;

* Local industry professionals;
* Professors and researchers in the field of industrial automation and AI.

13. OBJECTIVES

13.1. GENERAL OBJECTIVE

The overall aim of this project is to promote integration between the university and the local industrial community through extension activities aimed at implementing artificial intelligence (AI) systems for automating manufacturing processes, quality control and production optimization.

13.2. SPECIFIC OBJECTIVES

In order to achieve the main objective of this extension project, the specific objectives listed below were stipulated:

* Disseminate knowledge about AI and Industry 4.0.
* Train industry professionals in AI techniques applied to process automation.
* Develop partnerships between the university and companies in the industrial sector.
* Holding workshops and seminars on the practical application of AI in industry.

14. JUSTIFICATION AND RELEVANCE

The justification and relevance of this extension project are multifaceted and cover both academic and practical and social aspects.

* **Meeting the demands of industry and the community:** Industrial automation and the use of artificial intelligence are growing trends in modern industry. This project directly addresses these needs, training professionals and

students to deal with the current and future demands of the local industrial sector.

- **Integration between university and industry:** Promoting close collaboration between academia and business is essential to boosting innovation and regional economic development. By establishing partnerships and carrying out joint activities, the project strengthens ties between the university and the local industrial community.

- **Training qualified human resources:** By offering training in artificial intelligence techniques applied to industry, the project contributes to the training of highly qualified professionals, prepared to face the challenges of today's job market and contribute to technological and economic advancement.

- **Reducing costs and increasing efficiency:** The implementation of intelligent automation systems in partner companies results in a reduction in waste, increased productivity and improved product quality, which can have a positive impact on the companies' financial results and, consequently, on the local economy.

- **Transfer of knowledge and innovation:** The project promotes the transfer of academic knowledge to the industrial environment, enabling the practical application of innovative concepts and technologies. This can stimulate the creation of new solutions and practices in local industry, boosting competitiveness and sustainable development.

In this line of reasoning, the extension project is justified by its ability to meet the demands of industry, promote integration between university and industry, train qualified human resources, reduce costs and increase efficiency, and promote the transfer of knowledge and innovation, resulting in benefits for both academia and the industrial community and society as a whole.

15. THEORETICAL BACKGROUND

15.1. INDUSTRY 4.0

Industry 4.0, also known as the Fourth Industrial Revolution, represents a profound transformation in industrial processes, driven by the integration of advanced digital technologies. It is characterized by the fusion of cyber-physical systems, the Internet of Things (IoT), big data and artificial intelligence (AI), creating smart and highly connected factories (LEE et al., 2018).

The concept of Industry 4.0 emerged in Germany as part of a strategic plan to modernize manufacturing and increase global competitiveness. This new industrial era aims to automate and digitize production processes, allowing for greater flexibility, efficiency and mass customization of products (ZHOU et al., 2015).

One of the main characteristics of Industry 4.0 is the ability to collect and analyze data in real time, using sensors and connected devices to monitor and optimize each stage of production. AI plays a crucial role in this context, providing control systems and predictive analysis that help anticipate problems and improve product quality (LU, 2017).

The integration of these technologies results in a significant increase in productivity and operational efficiency, while reducing the waste of resources and improving the sustainability of industrial operations. Intelligent automation, through neural networks and deep learning algorithms, enables the identification of patterns and anomalies, optimizing quality control and decision-making (LEE et al., 2018).

In short, Industry 4.0 represents a significant advance in the way industrial processes are managed and executed, offering unprecedented opportunities for innovation and continuous improvement.

15.2. ARTIFICIAL INTELLIGENCE

Artificial Intelligence (AI) is a field of computer science dedicated to developing systems capable of performing tasks that traditionally require human intelligence. These tasks range from analyzing data to making complex decisions. AI seeks to replicate the capacity for learning, reasoning, problem-solving and decision-making that characterizes human thought.

One of the most fascinating features of AI is its ability to learn from data. This ability is exploited through techniques such as Machine Learning, which allows systems to improve their performance in certain tasks as they are exposed to more data. Another crucial technique is the use of Artificial Neural Networks, which are computer models inspired by the structure of the human brain and are capable of learning complex patterns in data.

In industry, AI is playing an increasingly important role in automating processes and optimizing production. Machine Learning, for example, can be applied to predict market demands, optimize supply chains and even prevent equipment failures. Artificial Neural Networks are used in quality control systems, identifying patterns in images and videos, and in diagnostic and predictive maintenance processes.

In addition, other AI techniques such as Natural Language Processing (NLP) are used to analyze texts and human-machine interaction through natural language. This makes it possible, for example, to automate customer service processes and extract insights from large volumes of textual data.

Computer Vision is another powerful technique that allows machines to understand and interpret the visual world, and is used in object recognition systems, product fault detection, and even autonomous vehicles.

In short, Artificial Intelligence is revolutionizing industry by offering tools and techniques capable of automating processes, increasing operational efficiency and providing valuable insights from data, thus contributing to the advancement and competitiveness of businesses in an increasingly digitalized world.

AI is therefore increasingly important in various areas of modern society due to its ability to transform processes, improve efficiency and promote innovation. It has become a significant driving force in several areas, including industry, health, finance and transportation.

Here are some aspects that highlight the importance of AI today (BRYNJOLFSSON; MCAFEE, 2014; RUSSELL; NORVIG, 2020; DOMINGOS, 2015):

- **Process automation:** AI makes it possible to automate repetitive and routine tasks, allowing human workers to focus on more complex and creative activities. This is particularly relevant in sectors such as manufacturing, where automation can significantly increase productivity and reduce errors.

- **Improved Decision Making:** AI systems are capable of analyzing large volumes of data in real time, offering insights that help with strategic decision-making. In sectors such as finance, health and logistics, this can lead to more informed and accurate decisions.

- **Personalization of Services:** AI enables the personalization of services on an unprecedented scale. For example, in digital marketing, AI algorithms can analyze consumer behavior and offer personalized recommendations, increasing customer satisfaction and sales.

- **Advances in Health:** In the field of health, AI is revolutionizing the diagnosis and treatment of diseases. Machine learning algorithms can analyze medical images to detect diseases more accurately and at earlier stages than traditional methods. In addition, AI is being used to develop personalized treatments and new drugs.

- **Improving Security:** AI plays a crucial role in cyber security, helping to detect and respond to threats in real time. In addition, AI-equipped surveillance systems can improve public safety by analyzing video in real time to identify suspicious behavior.

- **Economic Impact:** AI has a significant impact on the global economy, driving innovation and competitiveness. Companies that adopt AI can gain significant competitive advantages by increasing operational efficiency and creating new business models.

- **Education and Research:** AI is transforming education by personalizing learning for each student. Adaptive learning platforms use AI to identify students' individual needs and offer specific content to improve learning.

- **Industry 4.0:** In the context of Industry 4.0, AI is key to creating smart factories. AI systems can monitor and optimize operations in real time, predict equipment failures and improve product quality, resulting in greater efficiency and less waste.

In short, AI is playing a crucial role in technological advancement and the transformation of multiple sectors, bringing benefits ranging from improved operational efficiency to the personalization of services and advances in healthcare. Its continued implementation promises to shape the future in significant ways.

15.3. APPLICATION OF ARTIFICIAL INTELLIGENCE IN INDUSTRY 4.0

In the context of Industry 4.0, AI is key to intelligent automation and the creation of connected and efficient factories, among other applications such as:

- **Real-time monitoring:** AI enables continuous monitoring of industrial processes, identifying anomalies and patterns that may indicate future problems or opportunities for improvement (LEE et al., 2018);

- **Production Optimization:** Deep learning algorithms can optimize production processes, adjusting parameters in real time to maximize efficiency and minimize waste (ZHOU et al., 2015);

- **Quality Control:** AI can be used to inspect products accurately, ensuring high quality standards and reducing costs associated with defects (LU, 2017);

- **Predictive Maintenance:** With predictive analytics, AI can predict equipment failures before they occur, enabling proactive maintenance and reducing downtime (JESCHKE et al., 2017);

- **Automation and Efficiency:** AI enables the automation of repetitive and complex tasks, increasing efficiency and reducing human error. This is essential for competitiveness in a globalized market (MCKINSEY; COMPANY, 2018);

- **Data Analysis:** With the ability to process large volumes of data in real time, AI provides valuable insights that can improve decision-making and product innovation (BIESINGER et al., 2020);

- **Innovation:** AI drives innovation by enabling new ways of solving problems, from predicting failures to developing customized products (RUSSELL; NORVIG, 2021).

In short, AI is a crucial component of Industry 4.0, offering benefits ranging from automation and optimization of production processes to continuous innovation and quality improvement. Its application in industry transforms not only internal operations, but also the way companies interact with the market and adapt to change.

15.4. INDUSTRIAL AUTOMATION

Industrial Automation represents a significant advance in the way companies operate and manage their production processes. It involves the use of systems and technologies to control and operate industrial processes in an automated way, reducing the need for direct human intervention. This field covers a wide range of applications, from controlling simple processes to operating entire factories autonomously (HE et al., 2020).

There are different types of industrial automation, each with its own objectives and specific applications. Process automation refers to the automation of sequential and repetitive steps in a production line, such as the assembly of components in a car factory. Machine automation refers to the incorporation of automatic devices into industrial equipment to perform specific tasks, such as welding robots in metal production lines. Control automation deals with the automated monitoring and management of industrial processes, ensuring that they operate within predefined and safe parameters (SCHWABACHER; GOEBEL, 2007).

The advantages of industrial automation are diverse and have a positive impact on companies' efficiency and competitiveness. Firstly, automation helps to reduce operating costs by eliminating the need for human labor in repetitive and error-prone tasks. In addition, automation increases productivity by allowing machines to perform tasks faster and more efficiently than human workers (LIU et al., 2019).

Improving product quality is another significant advantage of industrial automation. By replacing manual intervention with automated processes, automation reduces variability and human error, resulting in more consistent and better quality products. In addition, automation provides greater operational flexibility, allowing companies to quickly adjust production to meet market demands and introduce new products more quickly (LEE et al., 2018).

Finally, industrial automation also contributes to safety in the workplace, reducing workers' exposure to dangerous environments and minimizing the risk of accidents. By implementing robust and reliable automation systems, companies can guarantee a safer and healthier working environment for their employees (BOGUE, 2017).

In short, industrial automation is a powerful tool for increasing efficiency, quality and safety in production processes, resulting in tangible benefits for companies and the economy as a whole. By adopting automation technologies, companies can remain competitive in an increasingly dynamic and demanding global market.

15.5. INDUSTRIAL AUTOMATION USING ARTIFICIAL INTELLIGENCE

Intelligent automation of industrial processes has become a fundamental pillar in Industry 4.0, leveraging advances in Artificial Intelligence to transform manufacturing operations. Industry 4.0, characterized by the integration of digital technologies into industrial processes, promises to optimize production, improve product quality and reduce waste. The use of AI, specifically neural networks and deep learning algorithms, makes it possible to identify patterns and anomalies in real time, which is essential for advanced automation and quality control.

Intelligent industrial automation involves using AI systems to automate tasks that previously required human intervention. This includes monitoring and controlling manufacturing processes to ensure that products are manufactured with high quality and efficiency. According to Lee et al. (2018), the application of neural networks in industrial processes has demonstrated a significant ability to predict failures and optimize the operation of equipment, which directly contributes to improving operational efficiency.

One of the main components of this transformation is the use of *deep learning*, which allows AI systems to learn from large volumes of data from sensors and other IoT (Internet of Things) devices. This is vital for the early detection of anomalies and predictive maintenance, areas where AI can predict problems before they occur and thus minimize machine downtime (SCHWABACHER; GOEBEL, 2007).

In addition, integrating AI into manufacturing processes facilitates real-time optimization, automatically adjusting operating parameters to maximize efficiency. This dynamic adjustment capability is essential for responding quickly to production variables and market demand (HE et al., 2020). An interdisciplinary approach, combining knowledge of production engineering and industrial wood engineering, is crucial to developing practical and effective solutions in the context of Industry 4.0.

In the area of quality control, convolutional neural networks (CNNs) have been widely used for product inspection, ensuring that each item produced meets established standards. Liu et al. (2019) point out that CNNs can detect defects on material surfaces with greater accuracy than traditional methods, demonstrating the potential of AI to revolutionize industrial quality control.

The development of AI systems for intelligent automation must also consider scalability and integration with existing systems. This involves creating flexible platforms that can be adapted to the specific needs of different industries. According to Bogue (2017), modularity and interoperability are critical aspects that must be incorporated into the design of automation solutions to ensure their broad and sustainable applicability.

In short, the intelligent automation of industrial processes, based on AI and Industry 4.0 technologies, represents a significant advance in modern manufacturing. The implementation of these technologies promises not only to increase productivity and efficiency, but also to reduce waste, promote sustainability and improve product quality. Studies and practical applications in various industrial sectors confirm the transformative potential of these innovations, paving the way for a future of smarter, more integrated production.

16. METHODOLOGY

The methodology adopted in this extension project is outlined in structured stages, which are fundamental to guaranteeing the effectiveness and success of the proposed extension activities, as well as achieving the established objectives.

16.1. NEEDS ASSESSMENT

•   Conducting a survey of companies in the local industrial community to identify the main needs and challenges related to process automation, quality control and production optimization.

16.2. DEVELOPMENT OF TEACHING MATERIALS

•   Preparation of comprehensive teaching material on AI and Industry 4.0, including texts, presentations, videos and case studies, with accessible language and practical examples aimed at the industrial context.

16.3. PLANNING AND EXECUTION OF WORKSHOPS AND SEMINARS

•   Planning workshops and seminars in person and/or online, with the participation of university experts and industry professionals, covering relevant topics on AI and its application in industry.

•   Wide dissemination of the events to local companies, encouraging participation and engagement of interested professionals.

16.4. TRAINING IN ARTIFICIAL INTELLIGENCE TECHNIQUES

•   Training courses in AI techniques applied to process automation, covering topics such as Machine Learning, Artificial Neural Networks, Natural Language Processing and Computer Vision.

•   Use of active teaching methodologies, such as case studies and practical projects, to promote the application of the concepts learned.

16.5. ESTABLISHING PARTNERSHIPS

- Identification and establishment of strategic partnerships between the university and companies in the industrial sector, aimed at mutual collaboration in the implementation of AI projects and the sharing of resources and knowledge.

16.6. DEVELOPMENT OF PILOT PROJECTS

- Development of pilot projects to implement AI systems in partner companies, addressing real cases of manufacturing process automation, quality control and production optimization.
- Close monitoring of pilot projects, offering technical support and making adjustments as necessary.

16.7. EVALUATION AND MONITORING

- Continuous evaluation of the impact of the activities carried out, both at the university and in the partner companies, using previously established performance indicators.
- Monitoring the development of skills and abilities of professionals trained in AI, as well as the progress of implemented projects.

This methodology aims to achieve the proposed objectives by promoting integration between the university and the local industrial community, disseminating knowledge about AI and Industry 4.0, training industry professionals, developing strategic partnerships and promoting the practical application of AI in industry through workshops, seminars and pilot projects.

17. COHERENCE BETWEEN OBJECTIVE, THEORETICAL BASIS AND METHODOLOGY

The coherence between the objectives, the theoretical basis and the methodology is the essential foundation for the success of the extension project presented, which aims to promote integration between the university and the local industrial community through the implementation of artificial intelligence (AI) systems in industry.

The project's objectives have been carefully designed to reflect its main mission: to disseminate knowledge about AI and Industry 4.0, to train industry professionals in AI techniques applied to process automation, to develop partnerships between the university and companies in the industrial sector, and to hold workshops and seminars on the practical application of AI in industry. These objectives provide a clear and specific direction for all the activities to be carried out throughout the project.

The theoretical foundation, in turn, is essential to provide a conceptual basis for the proposed objectives. Based on a comprehensive review of the literature on AI, Industry 4.0 and industrial automation, the project benefits from a solid theoretical framework that supports the importance and feasibility of the planned actions. Fundamental concepts such as machine learning, artificial neural networks and natural language processing are explored to provide a solid knowledge base that guides the development and implementation of the project's activities.

The methodology adopted directly reflects the objectives set and the theoretical basis presented. Through carefully planned stages, such as needs assessment, development of teaching material, planning and execution of workshops and seminars, training in AI techniques, establishment of strategic partnerships and development of pilot projects, the project aims to achieve its objectives in a systematic and effective way. The methodology provides a clear and comprehensive framework for implementing the proposed actions, ensuring a consistent approach in line with the project's objectives and theoretical foundation.

Thus, coherence between objectives, theoretical foundation and methodology is essential to ensure that the extension project achieves its goals of promoting integration between the university and the local industrial community, disseminating knowledge about AI, training industry professionals, developing strategic partnerships and promoting the practical application of AI in industry. By integrating these elements in a cohesive and harmonious way, the project can achieve significant results and contribute to the advancement of knowledge and innovation in local industry.

18. ADEQUACY AND RELEVANCE OF UNIVERSITY EXTENSION ACTIVITIES IN RELATION TO THE TARGET AUDIENCE

The university extension actions proposed in the project are directly appropriate and relevant to the target audience identified, which is made up of production engineering and industrial wood engineering students, local industry professionals, and professors and researchers in the field of industrial automation and AI. Each of these actions has been carefully planned to meet the specific needs of this audience and provide tangible and significant benefits.

For students of production engineering and industrial wood engineering, outreach activities offer a unique opportunity to improve their skills and knowledge in relation to the latest technologies and industry practices. The workshops, seminars and training courses in AI techniques applied to process automation provide a solid foundation for their academic training and preparation for the job market, enabling them to acquire skills that are highly valued by the industrial sector.

For local industry professionals, the outreach activities provide an opportunity for professional updating and improvement, enabling them to effectively implement and use AI systems in their operations. The workshops and seminars on the practical application of AI in industry provide valuable insights and practical tools to improve the efficiency, quality and competitiveness of local companies, allowing them to keep up to date with the latest trends and technologies in the sector.

For professors and researchers in the field of industrial automation and AI, outreach activities offer an opportunity to collaborate and exchange knowledge with the local industrial sector. The development of partnerships between the university and companies in the industrial sector makes it possible to carry out applied research projects and transfer knowledge and technologies between academia and industry, promoting effective integration between theory and practice and stimulating innovation and technological development.

In summary, the university extension actions proposed in the project are highly appropriate and relevant to the target audience identified, providing significant benefits both for the students, professionals and researchers involved, as well as for companies and the local industrial community as a whole. By offering opportunities for learning, training and collaboration, the project contributes to the advancement of knowledge and the sustainable development of regional industry.

19. INSEPARABILITY BETWEEN TEACHING, RESEARCH AND EXTENSION

The inseparability of teaching, research and extension is a fundamental principle that permeates the extension project mentioned, reflecting the interdependence and complementarity of these three dimensions in the academic context. In this specific project, the integration of teaching, research and extension is essential to achieving the proposed objectives and promoting a symbiotic relationship between the university and the local industrial community.

Firstly, the teaching dimension is present through the training and education activities offered to production engineering and industrial wood engineering students. The workshops, seminars and training courses in AI techniques applied to process automation provide a unique opportunity for practical and applied learning, integrating the theoretical concepts learned in the classroom with real industry experiences.

Research also plays a key role in the project, providing the theoretical and methodological basis for the development of outreach activities. The literature review on AI, Industry 4.0 and industrial automation serves as a starting point for identifying knowledge gaps and innovation opportunities, guiding the development of strategies and actions that seek effective and applicable solutions to the challenges faced by local industry.

Finally, university extension is the link that connects the knowledge generated by research and the academic training offered by teaching with the needs and demands of the local industrial community. Extension activities, such as workshops, seminars and pilot projects to implement AI systems, promote the transfer of knowledge and technologies between universities and companies, stimulating innovation, economic and social development and improving the quality of life in the region.

Thus, the inseparability between teaching, research and extension in the extension project in question is essential to promote a holistic and integrated approach to education and technological development, contributing to the training of qualified professionals, the generation of scientific knowledge and the practical application of this knowledge to benefit society as a whole.

20. EXECUTION SCHEDULE

Below is a detailed one-year timetable for the extension actions presented in the project methodology:

MONTH 1-2: LITERATURE REVIEW AND INITIAL PLANNING
- A literature review on AI, Industry 4.0 and industrial automation.
- Define specific project objectives.
- Establish partnerships with local companies.
- Planning extension activities and setting targets.
- Identify the resources needed.

MONTH 3-4: DEVELOPMENT OF TEACHING MATERIALS AND DISSEMINATION
- Developing teaching material for workshops and seminars.
- Preparing presentations, case studies and support materials.
- Start publicizing the events to the target audience.

- Establish contact with potential speakers and collaborators.

MONTH 5-6: WORKSHOPS AND SEMINARS

- Holding workshops and seminars on AI and Industry 4.0.
- Cover topics such as the practical application of AI in industry, process automation and quality control.
- Provide training in AI techniques for local industry professionals.
- To promote networking between students, professionals and researchers.

MONTH 7-8: DATA COLLECTION AND PRE-PROCESSING

- Collect data from partner companies to develop case studies.
- Preparing data for analysis and model development.
- Carry out preliminary data analysis and identify trends.

MONTH 9-10: DEVELOPING AI MODELS

- Use machine learning techniques and neural networks to create AI models.
- Test and validate the models with simulated data.
- Adjust the models based on the results obtained.

MONTH 11-12: IMPLEMENTATION AND INTEGRATION

- Integrating AI models into the manufacturing processes of partner companies.
- Carry out practical demonstrations and offer technical support.
- Evaluate the effectiveness of the models implemented.
- Prepare final report and present results.

This detailed schedule distributes the activities over the course of a year, ensuring that each stage of the project is properly planned and executed within the established timeframe.

21. MATERIALS AND FINANCIAL RESOURCES BUDGET

In order to carry out this extension project, various materials and resources will be needed. Here is a list of the main ones:

- **Teaching material:** Preparation of presentations, case studies and support materials for workshops and seminars. **Estimated cost:** R$ 20,000.00.

- **Infrastructure for events:** Physical space for workshops and seminars, with audiovisual and projection equipment. **Estimated cost:** R$ 50,000.00.

- **Human Resources:** Remuneration of speakers and facilitators for workshops and seminars. Costs associated with hiring staff to organize and coordinate activities. Scholarships for undergraduate and postgraduate students. **Estimated cost:** R$180,000.00.

- **Technology and Software:** High-performance computers for training AI models. Data analysis and AI development software. **Estimated cost:** R$100,000.00.

- **Financial Resources for Pilot Projects:** Funding **for** pilot projects to implement AI systems in partner companies. **Estimated cost:** R$150,000.00.

- **Marketing and** publicity: Costs associated with publicizing the events, such as printing promotional materials, online advertising and logistics costs. **Estimated cost:** R$ 30,000.00.

- **Logistics and Travel:** Costs associated with travel to establish partnerships with companies, carry out technical visits and take part in events related to the project. **Estimated cost:** R$ 70,000.00.

TOTAL: R$ 600,000.00.

This hypothetical distribution of the budget considers a balanced allocation of resources to ensure that all the activities planned in the extension project are carried out. However, the amounts may vary depending on the specific needs and priorities of the project. It is therefore essential to review and adjust the budget as necessary during the course of the project.

22. LEVEL OF FEASIBILITY

This extension project will be carried out by a team made up of research professors, laboratory technicians and undergraduate and postgraduate students from UNESP - Câmpus Itapeva.

The level of feasibility of this extension project is considered to be high, given the characteristics of the planned activities and the availability of adequate financial resources for its execution. Several reasons support this positive assessment:

- **Clarity of Objectives:** The project's objectives are well-defined and specific, which makes it easier to devise strategies and make decisions during implementation.

- **Solid Theoretical Basis:** The project has a robust theoretical basis, derived from a literature review on AI, Industry 4.0 and industrial automation. This provides an in-depth understanding of the topic and guides the development of the activities.

- **Structured Methodology:** The proposed **methodology** presents a logical and detailed sequence of steps and actions to be carried out throughout the project. This guarantees a systematic and efficient approach to achieving the proposed objectives.

- **Adequate financial resources:** The project has a significant financial budget, which makes it possible to invest in the materials, infrastructure, human resources and technology needed to carry it out. This increases the viability of the planned activities.

- **Support from the Local Industrial Community:** The partnership established with companies in the local industrial sector shows the community's interest in and support for the project, which can facilitate collaboration and the realization of the proposed activities.

- **Potential Impact:** The proposed extension actions have the potential to generate significant positive impacts, both in the academic training of students and in improving the processes and competitiveness of local companies.

Considering these aspects, the project demonstrates a high level of feasibility, with a solid structure and adequate resources for its execution. However, it is important to maintain efficient management, monitoring the project's progress and making adjustments as necessary to ensure that the proposed objectives are achieved within the established timeframe and budget.

23. LEVEL OF VISIBILITY

The level of visibility of this extension project is considered to be high, due to its relevance both within the academic community and in the context of local industry. Several characteristics contribute to this high visibility:

- **Impact on the Academic Community:** The project involves students, teachers and researchers, promoting effective integration between academic knowledge and practical application in industry. This interaction between the university and the academic community strengthens institutional ties and stimulates scientific and technological production.

- **Collaboration with Industry:** The partnership established with companies in the local industrial sector extends the project's reach and visibility. By promoting the implementation of artificial intelligence (AI) systems in industry, the project contributes to innovation and technological development in the sector, which attracts the attention of other companies and organizations interested in adopting similar practices.

- **Public Events and Activities:** The workshops, seminars and pilot projects carried out as part of the project provide opportunities for disseminating knowledge and exchanging experiences with a wide audience. These public events increase the visibility of the project and allow its results to be shared and debated with the wider community.

- **Repercussion in the Media and Social Networks:** The project's activities and achievements have the potential to attract the attention of local and specialized media, generating coverage and reports that increase its visibility. In addition, active promotion on social networks and other communication channels helps to disseminate the project's achievements and attract interest to its initiatives.

- **Potential for replication and scale:** The results achieved by the project, such as the successful implementation of intelligent automation systems and the reduction of waste in partner industries, have the potential to inspire and influence other institutions and companies to adopt similar practices. This increases the impact and visibility of the project, as its ideas and experiences are shared and replicated in different contexts.

As a result, the extension project has a high level of visibility, both within the academic community and in industry and society in general. Its relevance and impact are recognized and highlighted, which contributes to its consolidation as an outstanding initiative in the field of artificial intelligence and industrial automation.

24. EXPECTED RESULTS

The expected results of this extension project are diverse and wide-ranging, reflecting the objectives set and the activities planned. These results are in line with the project's mission to promote integration between the university and the local industrial community through the implementation of artificial intelligence (AI) systems for automating manufacturing processes, quality control and production optimization. The main expected results include:

- **Training Professionals and Students:** The project is expected to train local industry professionals and engineering students in AI techniques applied to process automation. This includes developing the practical skills and theoretical understanding needed to effectively apply AI concepts in industry.

- **Successful Implementation of Intelligent Automation Systems:** The project aims at the practical implementation of intelligent automation systems in partner companies. These systems are expected to improve operational efficiency, product quality and the competitiveness of companies, resulting in tangible benefits such as reduced costs and increased productivity.

- **Waste Reduction and Production Optimization:** With the implementation of AI systems, it is expected that there will be a significant reduction in waste and optimization of production processes in partner industries.

This can include identifying opportunities for improvement, optimizing workflows and preventing process failures.

- **Strengthening University-Company Partnerships:** The project aims to establish and strengthen partnerships between universities and companies in the industrial sector. It is hoped that this collaboration will result in mutual benefits, such as sharing knowledge and technology, carrying out applied research projects and training qualified professionals.

- **Promoting Innovation in Industry:** Finally, the project is expected to promote innovation in local industry, encouraging the adoption of new technologies and advanced automation practices. This can contribute to the economic and social development of the region, as well as positioning the partner companies as leaders in their sectors.

In summary, the expected results of this extension project are broad and significant, reflecting its potential impact on industry and the local community. Through training, the implementation of advanced technologies and the strengthening of partnerships, the project aims to promote a positive transformation in the processes and competitiveness of companies, as well as contributing to the advancement of knowledge and innovation in the area of industrial automation and artificial intelligence.

REFERENCES

BIESINGER, F.; WEYRICH, M.; MEISEN, T. **Artificial Intelligence in Industry 4.0 and its Impact on Supply Chains**. Procedia CIRP, v. 93, p. 161-165, 2020.

BOGUE, R. **What are the prospects for robots in the factory? Part 1**. Industrial Robot: An International Journal, 2017.

BRYNJOLFSSON, E.; MCAFEE, A. **The Second Machine Age**: Work, Progress, and Prosperity in a Time of Brilliant Technologies. New York: W.W. Norton & Company, 2014.

DOMINGOS, P. **The Master Algorithm**: How the Quest for the Ultimate Learning Machine Will Remake Our World. New York: Basic Books, 2015.

GOODFELLOW, I.; BENGIO, Y.; COURVILLE, A. **Deep Learning**. Cambridge: MIT Press, 2016.

HASTIE, T.; TIBSHIRANI, R.; FRIEDMAN, J. **The Elements of Statistical Learning**: Data Mining, Inference, and Prediction. 2. ed. New York: Springer, 2009.

HE, Y.; XU, X.; WANG, Z.; JIANG, Y. **Predictive Maintenance in Smart Manufacturing**: A Review. IEEE Transactions on Industrial Informatics, 2020.

HUGHES, T. J. **The Finite Element Method**: Linear Static and Dynamic Finite Element Analysis. 2. ed. New York: Courier Corporation, 2012.

JESCHKE, S.; BRECHER, C.; MEISEN, T.; ÖZDEMIR, D.; ESCHERT, T. **Industrial Internet of Things and Cyber Manufacturing Systems**. New York: Springer, 2017.

JORDAN, M. I.; MITCHELL, T. M. **Machine Learning**: Trends, Perspectives, and Prospects. Science, v. 349, n. 6245, p. 255-260, 2015.

KAGERMANN, H.; WAHLSTER, W.; HELBIG, J. **Recommendations for Implementing the Strategic Initiative INDUSTRIE 4.0**: Securing the Future of German Manufacturing Industry. 2013.

KAGERMANN, H.; WAHLSTER, W.; HELBIG, J. **Recommendations for Implementing the Strategic Initiative INDUSTRIE 4.0**. Final Report of the Industrie 4.0 Working Group, 2013.

KUSIAK, A. **Smart Manufacturing**. International Journal of Production Research, v. 56, n. 1-2, p. 508-517, 2018.

LECUN, Y.; BENGIO, Y.; HINTON, G. **Deep Learning**. Nature, v. 521, n. 7553, p. 436-444, 2015.

LEE, J.; BAGHERI, B.; KAO, H. A. **A Cyber-Physical Systems Architecture for Industry 4.0-Based Manufacturing Systems**. Manufacturing Letters, v. 3, p. 18-23, 2018.

LIU, C.; LIU, P.; JIANG, L. **Surface Defect Detection of Industrial Products Based on Deep Learning**. Journal of Intelligent Manufacturing, 2019.

MCKINSEY & COMPANY. **Artificial Intelligence**: The Next Digital Frontier?. 2018.

OSBORNE, M. J.; RUBINSTEIN, A. **A Course in Game Theory**. Cambridge: MIT Press, 1994.

RUSSELL, S.; NORVIG, P. **Artificial Intelligence**: A Modern Approach. 4. ed. New York: Pearson, 2020.

RUSSELL, S.; NORVIG, P. **Artificial Intelligence**: A Modern Approach. 5. ed. New York: Pearson, 2021.

SCHMIDHUBER, J. **Deep Learning in Neural Networks**: An Overview. Neural Networks, v. 61, p. 85-117, 2015.

SCHWABACHER, M.; GOEBEL, K. **A Survey of Artificial Intelligence for Prognostics**. AAAI Fall Symposium - Technical Report, 2007.

WANG, S.; WAN, J.; LI, D.; ZHANG, C. **Implementing Smart Factory of Industrie 4.0**: An Outlook. International Journal of Distributed Sensor Networks, v. 12, n. 1, p. 3159805, 2016.

ZHANG, Y.; REN, S.; LIU, Y.; SI, S. **A Big Data Analytics Architecture for Cleaner Manufacturing and Maintenance Processes of Complex Products**. Journal of Cleaner Production, v. 142, p. 626-641, 2017.

ZHOU, K.; LIU, T.; ZHOU, L. **Industry 4.0**: Towards Future Industrial Opportunities and Challenges. In: 12th International Conference on Fuzzy Systems and Knowledge Discovery (FSKD). 2015. p. 2147-2152.

yes
I want morebooks!

Buy your books fast and straightforward online - at one of world's fastest growing online book stores! Environmentally sound due to Print-on-Demand technologies.

Buy your books online at
www.morebooks.shop

Kaufen Sie Ihre Bücher schnell und unkompliziert online – auf einer der am schnellsten wachsenden Buchhandelsplattformen weltweit! Dank Print-On-Demand umwelt- und ressourcenschonend produziert.

Bücher schneller online kaufen
www.morebooks.shop

MIX
Papier aus verantwortungsvollen Quellen
Paper from responsible sources
FSC® C105338

Printed by Books on Demand GmbH, Norderstedt / Germany